Pfeiffer™

COACHING FOR COMMITMENT WORKSHOP

PARTICIPANT WORKBOOK

THIRD EDITION

Cindy Coe

Amy Zehnder

Dennis Kinlaw

BICENTENNIAL
1807
WILEY
2007
BICENTENNIAL

John Wiley & Sons, Inc.

Copyright © 2008 by John Wiley & Sons, Inc. All Rights Reserved.

Published by Pfeiffer
An Imprint of Wiley
989 Market Street, San Francisco, CA 94103-1741
www.pfeiffer.com

No part of this publication may be reproduced, stored in a retrieval system, or transmitted in any form or by any means, electronic, mechanical, photocopying, recording, scanning, or otherwise, except as permitted under Section 107 or 108 of the 1976 United States Copyright Act, without either the prior written permission of the Publisher, or authorization through payment of the appropriate per-copy fee to the Copyright Clearance Center, Inc., 222 Rosewood Drive, Danvers, MA 01923, 978-750-8400, fax 978-646-8600, or on the web at www.copyright.com. Requests to the Publisher for permission should be addressed to the Permissions Department, John Wiley & Sons, Inc., 111 River Street, Hoboken, NJ 07030, 201-748-6011, fax 201-748-6008, or online at http://www.wiley.com/go/permissions.

Limit of Liability/Disclaimer of Warranty: While the publisher and author have used their best efforts in preparing this book, they make no representations or warranties with respect to the accuracy or completeness of the contents of this book and specifically disclaim any implied warranties of merchantability or fitness for a particular purpose. No warranty may be created or extended by sales representatives or written sales materials. The advice and strategies contained herein may not be suitable for your situation. You should consult with a professional where appropriate. Neither the publisher nor author shall be liable for any loss of profit or any other commercial damages, including but not limited to special, incidental, consequential, or other damages.

Readers should be aware that Internet websites offered as citations and/or sources for further information may have changed or disappeared between the time this was written and when it is read.

PowerPoint is a registered trademark of the Microsoft Corporation.

For additional copies/bulk purchases of this book in the U.S. please contact 800-274-4434.

Pfeiffer books and products are available through most bookstores. To contact Pfeiffer directly call our Customer Care Department within the U.S. at 800-274-4434, outside the U.S. at 317-572-3985, fax 317-572-4002, or visit www.pfeiffer.com.

Pfeiffer also publishes its books in a variety of electronic formats. Some content that appears in print may not be available in electronic books.

ISBN: 978-0-7879-8248-5
Acquiring Editor: Martin Delahoussaye
Director of Development: Kathleen Dolan Davies
Developmental Editor: Susan Rachmeler
Production Editor: Dawn Kilgore
Editor: Rebecca Taff
Editorial Assistant: Julie Rodriquez
Manufacturing Supervisor: Becky Morgan

Printed in the United States of America

Printing   10   9   8   7   6   5   4   3   2

CONTENTS

Coaching for Commitment Workshop Outline

Coaching for Commitment

 1 hour, 30 minutes

My Coaching Definition

Name _____

A cartoon character that represents me is:

_____

My Definition of Coaching

Be brief and succinct!

Coaching is. . .

_____

_____

_____

_____

_____

_____

_____

_____

_____

_____

Copy your definition onto a sticky note and place it on the "My Coaching Definition" easel pad.

 How many years have you been coaching based on your definition?

Shared Definition of Coaching

Coaching is all about the
person being coached (PBC)!

Successful coaching is a conversation of
self-discovery that follows a logical
process and leads to superior
performance, commitment to sustained
growth, and positive relationships.

Coaching Is. . .

Coaching Is	Coaching Is Not

MY CURRENT COACHING CULTURE

Currently, how is coaching used or perceived by my team and in my organization?

_____

_____

_____

_____

_____

_____

_____

_____

Great Expectations

During this workshop, you will have the opportunity to. . .

- Get **involved** by understanding the various roles you play when interacting with others.

- **Discover** ways to be more effective in the coach role, and how to gain commitment from the person being coached (PBC).

- **Commit** to Creating a Coaching for Commitment Culture.

Just as coaches who live and breathe coaching must sometimes make a conscious shift to a non-coaching role when dealing with others, non-coaches and new coaches alike must make a similar shift in thinking like a coach before approaching a coaching conversation.

This workshop may change the way you have always thought about coaching!

Coaching for Commitment

What does it take for me to be committed to something—family, career, goals, hobby, etc.?

_____

_____

_____

_____

_____

_____

_____

_____

_____

_____

_____

_____

_____

_____

_____

_____

_____

_____

Commitment, like motivation, is not something that you can observe directly. You infer that it exists because of what people do. We say that people are "committed" when they demonstrate over and over again their determination to do their best and their unwillingness to give up in the face of obstacles. Committed people in organizations are tied intellectually and emotionally to the values and goals of the organization. Committed people know what they are doing, and they believe that what they are doing is important. People cannot become committed to what is vague or trivial.

UNDERSTANDING HOW COACHING BUILDS COMMITMENT

People tend to become fully committed to do their best all of the time to the degree that they

- Are clear about core values and performance goals
- Have influence over what they do
- Have the competence to perform the jobs that are expected of them
- Are appreciated for their performance

CRITICAL CONDITIONS FOR BUILDING COMMITMENT

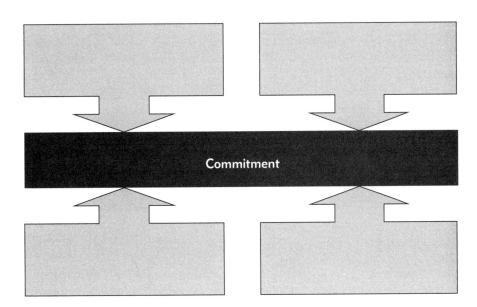

Being Clear

Clear about the organization's core values and its primary goals. When people are clear about the organization's values and goals, they can align their work to these goals, which in turn provides role clarity and a sense of belonging.

Ambivalence and confusion are the enemies of commitment. Knowing what the real values and goals of an organization are provides members a framework within which a vast variety of behaviors is possible.

Having Influence

Encourage people to exercise influence and explore and analyze the various problems they must solve at work and with their relationships with others. Every person in an organization is presented countless opportunities to influence others. This behavior needs to be encouraged. It takes discipline to encourage people to exert influence.

Commitment

Being Competent

People do not naturally want to fail, but they will often try to avoid the tasks that they think they cannot do. If you want commitment from people, you must ensure they have the tools, resources, ability, and willingness to succeed in their jobs. Two elements must be addressed when building competency in others: (1) You must ensure that people have the knowledge, skill, experience, tools, and resources to perform and (2) You must ensure that people have the confidence to perform. Coaching accomplishes both of these.

Feeling Appreciated

Everybody needs to feel appreciated. For what they do, say, think, feel, you name it. Appreciation is shown by the words people use and the behaviors they display to others. When someone feels that his or her ideas are appreciated, he or she will be more committed to them.

Overall Goal

BUILDING COMMITMENT THROUGH COACHING

Coaching for Commitment

Coaching is not a secret or a weapon and it is not something you do "to" people. It is something you do *with* people. Coaching is considered successful when people commit to their own ideas and put their words into action. More than that, your goal as a coach should be to commit to modeling the art of coaching through the use of the techniques and skills presented in this workbook. Imagine the power of many coaches working together to build commitment to sustained growth and superior performance.

Temperature Check

Current Reality: Use a 1 to 3 scale to answer the following questions.

1 = not committed at all   2 = somewhat committed   3 = totally committed

	Current Reality	Ideal State (Where should it be?)
What is your personal level of commitment to coaching?	1 2 3	1 2 3
What is your personal level of commitment to creating a coaching culture?	1 2 3	1 2 3
(if applicable) What is your manager's level of commitment to coaching?	1 2 3	1 2 3
(if applicable) What is your manager's level of commitment to creating a coaching culture?	1 2 3	1 2 3
(if applicable) What is your organization's level of commitment to coaching?	1 2 3	1 2 3
(if applicable) What is your organization's level of commitment to creating a coaching culture?	1 2 3	1 2 3

Ideal State: Where do you think the level of commitment should be for each?

Action Plan: What is your part in maintaining the current level (if above 1) or achieving a higher level? How can you influence others?

My Turn

My biggest learning from this module was. . .

_____

_____

_____

_____

_____

_____

_____

_____

_____

_____

_____

_____

_____

_____

_____

_____

_____

_____

_____

_____

_____

My Turn

2

The Coach Role

 2 hours

Module 2 Objectives

In this module, you will have the opportunity to. . .

- **Get involved** by assessing the role you gravitate toward most often.
- **Discover** your coaching gap.
- **Commit** to improving at least one skill that will help you to become a skillful coach.

In the world of coaching you must first know where you are, before you can get where you want to be!

Coaching Skills Inventory

 Wait! Please don't turn the page until instructed to do so. Complete the *Coaching Skills Inventory* (CSI) first, which will be provided by your facilitator.

Role Model

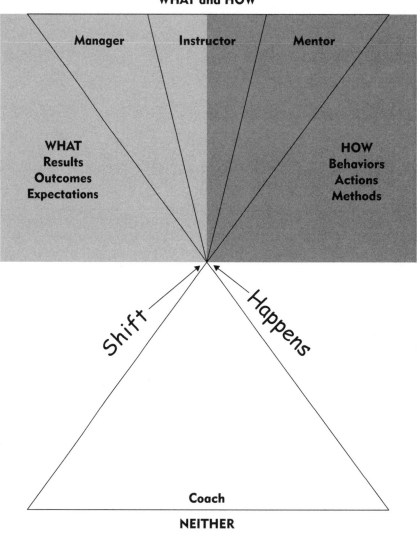

Shift Happens

The best coaches know when they are coaching. They know what techniques make what they do coaching versus some other role. Coaches make the mental shift to coach before conducting coaching conversations, and they are aware of using a coaching process during the conversation.

At that precise moment in time when you make the shift to the *coach role*, you should:

- Let go of *What* and *How*.
- Eliminate coaching biases.
- Be *egoless*.
- Eliminate mental and physical distractions:
    - Free your mind from distractions by continuously refocusing on the PBC and his or her needs. Use self-talk to help you.
    - Clear the clutter from your mind and workspace by turning off email, phones, and other distractions.
    - Whatever you do, don't multitask during your coaching conversations. Remain focused on the PBC.

COACHING BIASES

Coaching biases are coaching derailers!

No one will feel satisfied in a coaching conversation or relationship with you if he or she sense that he or she is being subjected to your whims and biases.

As soon as someone feels your biases or prejudices, you have lost your credibility as a coach and a leader.

Biases and prejudices stem from?

_____

_____

_____

_____

_____

What are my hot buttons?

_____

_____

_____

_____

_____

Remaining unbiased sounds like?
Example: "Tell me what you are thinking?"

_____

_____

_____

_____

_____

THE VALUES CHALLENGE

Your values are one of the many things that make you unique. Living by your values is easy. Expecting others to live by your values has about as much chance of success as your chances of winning the lottery. In coaching, one of your biggest challenges may be allowing others to live and work based on *their* values and not expecting or forcing them to think, act, live, or behave according to *yours*.

This presents a challenge for coaches!

Which of my values will I have the hardest time letting go of during coaching conversations?

_____

_____

EGOLESS

Being *Egoless* Means That YOU . . .

- Coach based on the needs of the PBC.
- Don't take things personally.
- Don't blame.
- Don't make assumptions.
- Take your own goals, drive, aspirations, and emotions out of the mix.
- Check your ego at the door.
- Bring the most unselfish, unbiased self you can to the table!

What does "being *egoless*" mean to me?

_____

_____

_____

What can I do to practice being *egoless*?

_____

_____

_____

Egoless means that, rather than being the rewarded problem solver or winner, you find ways to help elevate the PBC to that status.

Coach Role

PERSPECTIVES OF A COACH

What does a coach focus on?

1. _____

2. _____

3. _____

4. _____

5. _____

WHEN TO COACH?

The *coach role* is best used for interactions that move the PBC forward, specifically when the PBC:

- Needs insight about behavior and actions, sometimes gained through the use of 360-degree feedback assessments.
- Is feeling stagnant, stuck, or has outgrown a role.
- Has a drive for greatness.
- Is not sure what is interfering with the ability to achieve some personal or professional goal.
- Needs to find a way to move forward or make progress.
- Is trying to move from average or good to better and best.
- Realizes that some technical, organizational, or other problem is blocking his or her performance or potential.
- Has a very difficult choice to make, such as the decision to take on a new role or new challenge.
- Needs help preparing for an upcoming difficult conversation or presentation.

The *coach's role* is to help PBCs gain insight and understanding regarding the topic of conversation, not to solve problems for them. In coaching conversations, the coach spends the majority of time (80 percent) listening and the remaining time (20 percent) asking mostly open-ended coaching questions. Many coaches struggle with not solving or wanting to direct the conversation to their end and you too may find that this is very difficult to master. Coaching is also the role that most people believe they are using, when in reality they are not.

KNOW WHEN NOT TO COACH, TOO!

💣 Coaching ≠ Counseling

💣 Coaching ≠ Consulting

💣 Coaching ≠ Sports Coaching

Don't Pretend to Coach!

Don't pretend to be coaching when you're not. If you can't let go of WHAT and HOW, choose a different role. Not every conversation is a coaching conversation.

How do you know whether you are pretending to coach?

When you try to coach in the following situations, you probably should be using another role instead.

- If you want to maintain ownership of either the WHAT or the HOW.
- If you are trying to lead the person to your solutions or gain buy-in for your ideas.
- If it is about legal, procedural, or compliance issues.
- If you want the person to read your mind.

Recall a time in your life when someone was pretending to coach you. . . .

- What were you thinking?

  _____

  _____

  _____

- What was the outcome?

  _____

  _____

  _____

- What would have made the conversation/outcome more effective?

  _____

  _____

  _____

Simply Uncoachable

HOW DO I KNOW WHETHER THE PBC IS A TOUGH NUT OR A LOST CAUSE?

Tough Nuts are coachable, even though they present the most difficult coaching challenges you'll ever experience. Lost Causes, on the other hand, are simply uncoachable, which means you should use another role (*manager, mentor,* or *instructor*) to communicate with them.

The presence of several or more of these extreme traits would tend to classify your PBC as a lost cause (simply uncoachable):

Extreme Traits

- Constantly blames others, processes, procedures, or the environment for poor performance or behavior.
- Always plays the victim role.
- Doesn't respect his or her colleagues or you.
- Never takes personal accountability.
- Never takes on additional responsibilities.
- Rarely accomplishes assigned duties.
- Repeatedly refuses to be coached or says that he or she is not interested in coaching or development planning.
- Refuses to participate in the performance review process.
- Continually creates problems within the team.
- Has a diminished mental capacity to reason and process information or has a medical condition that would render him or her otherwise unable to reason or process information or cannot be held accountable for his or her actions.

Common Responses

- Combative.
- Disruptive.
- Uncommunicative.
- Defensive.
- Angry.
- Resentful.
- Asks for feedback and retaliates when it is given.

KNOW YOUR OPTIONS

Stop coaching and play a stronger manager role. Rather than continuing to try to coach, play a stronger manager role whenever dealing with this person. Tell this person WHAT you expect. You may even want to use the *Instructor* role and tell him or her WHAT you expect and HOW it will be accomplished. Either of these roles requires you to be more directive in your approach. Tell more than ask, or make assignments instead of asking for actions.

Take accountability for your role in the coaching relationship. Did you make a complete shift to coach? Did you let go of the WHAT and the HOW? Did you eliminate all biased comments and become *egoless*? Does a high level of trust exist between you and the PBC? If not, who is the untrusting party? Don't label the PBC as a lost cause if you have not played your part in shifting to the *coach role.*

Have your referral resources ready. If you have reason to believe the person is not coachable due to highly personal or mental health reasons, be prepared to suggest an employee assistance program, a therapist, or legal counsel if warranted. In addition, do not hesitate to contact one of these resources yourself if you are not sure how to handle the situation.

When dealing with human resource issues, strive to be *egoless* and objective, keeping your emotions and tone in check, and make your judgments on an objective basis. Observe and document inappropriate behaviors and actions. Do not hesitate to involve your HR representative early. They are highly skilled individuals who are trained to deal with such matters.

If the person is resistant but coachable, you may want to hire an external coach to work with him or her. Sometimes a new coach brings new perspectives and can be perceived as more objective. External coaches are not tied to internal politics, and this can be good. Exercise caution here because the last thing you want to do is bring in external coaches only to *fix* people. This will be counterproductive to the Coaching for Commitment Culture you are trying to create. If you are going to use external coaches, the general rule is to use them for your top performers as much as for your difficult ones.

WHEN HIRING AN EXTERNAL COACH

Here are some tips for hiring an external coach for your tough nuts:

- **Confront the person's behavior.**

- **Address the impact of the person's behavior.** What is the impact it is having on others, that person (tap into the intrinsic motivators), and the company?

- **Share the concept of coaching and its benefits.** Talk about what coaching is and what it can do and why a neutral party may be better suited to working with the person. Use the *Coaching for Commitment Discussion Guide* to assist you in explaining what coaching is.

- **Create a shared agenda for what the person will work on with the coach.** Either find a way to create a shared agenda about what should be worked on with a coach or be willing to let the potential PBC choose the agenda. Feel free to set terms such as he/she can only create his/her own agenda if it is based on 360-degree feedback, etc.

- **Get the PBC involved in selecting the right coach.** If you want results, don't pick a coach; let the person interview at least three coaches (internal or external) and select a coach, that is, the right fit for him or her. A good fit gets better results!

- **Agree on how feedback or updates will be communicated back to you and other stakeholders.** Your mutual feedback methodology should ensure coaching conversations between coach and PBC are totally confidential, while providing you with adequate information to note progress. Usually, the PBC is tasked with providing regular and honest progress reports to the manager. (Most coaches will not provide detailed progress reports unless otherwise designated in a coaching contract).

My Turn

My ah-ha from this module was. . .

_____

_____

_____

_____

_____

_____

_____

_____

_____

_____

_____

_____

_____

_____

_____

_____

_____

_____

_____

_____

_____

The Coaching Process

 30 minutes

Module 3 Objectives

In this module, you will have the opportunity to. . .

- **Get involved** by learning the Coaching Prism.
- **Discover** how all of the pieces come together.
- **Commit** to using the coaching process for your coaching conversations.

See the Light!

Focus on Coach Role

COACHING CHANNELS

Coaching conversations can happen using a number of methods.

- Face-to-Face
- Virtual:
  - Phone/Teleconference
  - Email
  - Video/Web Conference

The Coaching for Commitment techniques can be used effectively with any channel of coaching. Coaching outcomes can be just as powerful using virtual channels as with face-to-face methods.

Coaching Prism

THE COACHING PRISM IS THE ART OF COACHING

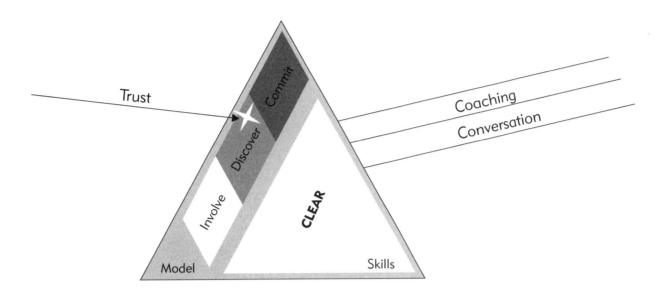

The Coaching Prism is similar in nature to any prism. White light goes in and a rainbow of seven colored lights comes out the other end. In the case of coaching, the white light is Trust and the rainbow is the coaching conversation. The complexity in between includes the coaching model and skills. Complex does not mean impossible. Complex can mean rich and amazing results.

Trust

Think of trust as the white light that enters the Coaching Prism. Trust is the primary catalyst and the first main component of all coaching conversations. Mutual trust between you and the PBC must be maintained throughout the coaching relationship. Without it, the PBC will not see the rainbow of light that is possible with coaching.

InDiCom Coaching Model

- InDiCom (pronounced In Dee Com) stands for the three phases of the coaching process: **In** = Involve; **Di** = Discover; and **Com** = Commit.

- It is a defined model, although it may not appear that way to the untrained eye. The model provides structure for the coaching conversation.

- It helps the coaching conversation feel like a natural conversation, not the purposeful process that it is.

- No matter how long or short coaching conversations are, they should consciously move through the defined model stages.

- The InDiCom model is designed to assist the PBC move from a current reality to an ideal state.

CLEAR Coaching Skills

Challenge

Listen

Encourage

Ask

Refine

- The CLEAR coaching skills are used with all phases of the InDiCom coaching model.

- They are common everyday communication skills from a coach's perspective designed to achieve maximum impact in a coaching conversation.

- Integrating these techniques into your skill set takes sustained effort, time, and practice.

The Coaching Conversation

- This is where everything comes together.

- You will combine the model, skills, and other techniques to conduct your coaching conversations.

- Coaching conversations should feel like fluid conversations. This is what makes coaching an art.

The Big Picture

By now you have learned what distinguishes the *coach role* from the roles of *manager, instructor*, and *mentor*, and you have seen the Coaching Prism, which defines the coaching process. The visual below illustrates how it all comes together into one big picture. Note how the Coaching Prism fits into the *coach role*.

BOTH
WHAT and HOW

| Manager | Instructor | Mentor |

WHAT
Results
Outcomes
Expectations

HOW
Behaviors
Actions
Methods

Trust

Shift

Commit

Happens

Coaching

Conversation

Discover

Involve

CLEAR

Model

Skills

Coach

NEITHER
WHAT nor HOW

My Turn

My ah-ha from this module was . . .

_____

_____

_____

_____

_____

_____

_____

_____

_____

_____

_____

_____

_____

_____

_____

_____

_____

_____

_____

_____

_____

4

Trust

 35 minutes

Module 4 Objectives

In this module, you will have the opportunity to. . .

- **Get involved**—Trust Me!

- **Discover** how to establish and maintain trust.

- **Commit** to using respectful behaviors.

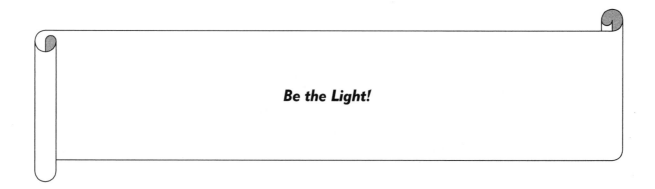

Be the Light!

Trust Me!

Identify characteristics and behaviors of people you *immediately* trust versus those of people you don't trust.

Trust	Don't Trust
_____	_____
_____	_____
_____	_____
_____	_____
_____	_____
_____	_____
_____	_____
_____	_____
_____	_____
_____	_____
_____	_____
_____	_____
_____	_____
_____	_____

Establishing and building trust is more than a skill. Trust is the most important aspect of coaching because every effective coaching relationship is built on a solid trust foundation.

Establishing and Maintaining Trust

In order to establish and build trust you must

- Be Honest.

- Be Authentic.

- Be Accountable.

- Be Respectful.

Establishing and maintaining trust requires sustained, conscious effort on the part of the coach. Remembering to be *egoless* is a great place to begin.

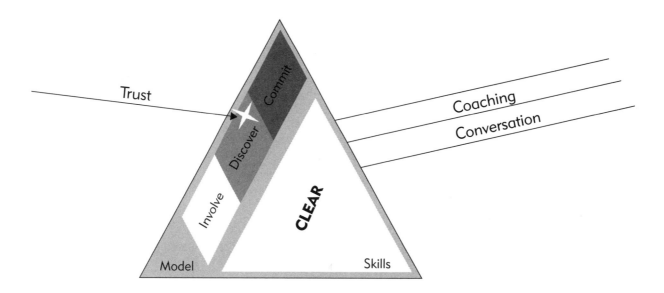

Trust adds the humanistic component to the coaching conversation. It assumes that the coach has genuine concern for the PBC, whether it is concern in wanting someone to succeed or concern for him or her as a person. It also assumes that the coach is comfortable in his or her own skin and operates from a place of genuineness instead of superficiality.

Respectful

What was the most *respectful* thing anyone ever said to you?

_____

_____

_____

_____

_____

_____

_____

What made it respectful?

_____

_____

_____

_____

_____

_____

_____

Trust and Respect Go Hand in Hand!

Disrespectful

What was the most *disrespectful* thing anyone ever said to you?

_____

_____

- How long ago did it happen?

_____

_____

- What feelings or emotions did you experience when it happened?

_____

_____

- What feelings or emotions do you experience when you think about it today?

_____

_____

- What is your level of trust with that person today?

_____

_____

- Would you want that person to be your coach?

_____

_____

- Why or why not?

_____

_____

"People may not remember what you did or what you said, but they will always remember how you made them feel."

—Author Unknown

Disrespectful Tone and Gestures

Many times your tone of voice, inflections, and gestures can be perceived as disrespectful. What tones and/or gestures have you used in the past that others could have perceived as disrespectful?

Level of Trust

You can measure the extent to which a trusting relationship exists by measuring the degree of influence that the PBC has during your coaching conversations.

Evaluate the level of trust in your coaching conversations by answering the following questions:

Question	Always				Not at All
I avoid using disrespectful tones, gestures, and sarcasm with the PBC.	5	4	3	2	1
I am honest in sharing my observations, not opinions, with the PBC.	5	4	3	2	1
I am respectful when I communicate with the PBC.	5	4	3	2	1
I encourage the PBC to take genuine ownership of the situation or problem and accountability for moving forward.	5	4	3	2	1
I take accountability for my part in issues with the PBC.	5	4	3	2	1
I am authentic and do not transfer my "baggage," insecurities, or issues to the PBC.	5	4	3	2	1

Although your self-assessment is important, keep in mind that the PBC's perception of the level of trust that exists is what really matters. Since a PBC's perception is reality, ask yourself if your PBCs would agree with your ratings.

Takeaway: For a broader view, mark this page for future reference and ask others to rate you.

My Turn

What insight will I take away from this module?

_____

_____

_____

_____

_____

_____

_____

_____

_____

_____

_____

_____

_____

_____

_____

_____

_____

_____

_____

_____

_____

_____

_____

5

The InDiCom Coaching Model

 2 hours, 55 minutes

Module 5 Objectives

In this module, you will have the opportunity to. . .

- **Get involved** by learning the InDiCom coaching model.

- **Discover** how the model works by learning the goals for each stage.

- **Commit** to using the InDiCom coaching model through practice, practice, practice.

*"You put your right foot in, You put your right foot out,
You put your right foot in. . ."*

—The Hokey Pokey

The InDiCom Coaching Model

Three stages make up the InDiCom coaching model

    Stage I: Involve

    Stage II: Discover

    Stage III: Commit

Certain goals must be met at each stage. These goals do not need to be completed in a checklist sort of way. Think of them as a guide as you walk through the coaching conversation.

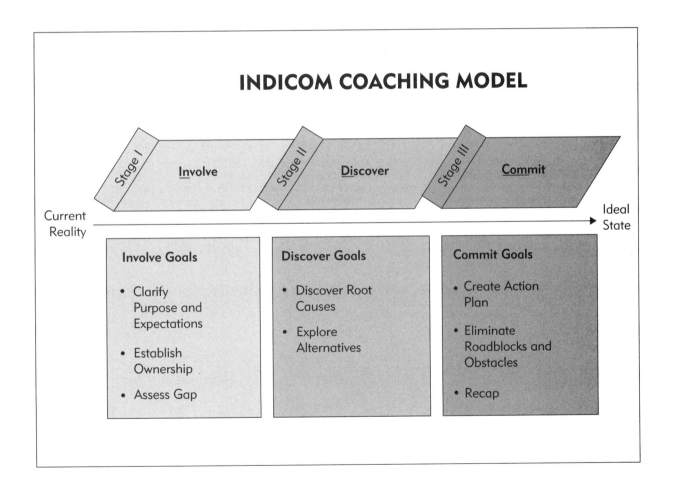

Coaching is a Process, not an Event!

Involve

During the Involve stage, you have three goals to achieve:

Clarify the Purpose and Expectations

- The purpose is identified by WHY the coaching conversation is occurring.

- Expectations are identified as outcomes, results, potential, or opportunity.

- The coach's primary role is to listen to what the PBC wants to discuss and assist in clarifying the issue.

Establish Ownership and Agreement

- Ownership describes the PBC's expressed willingness to assume the appropriate responsibility and take personal accountability for the situation at hand.

- The *coach's role* is to help the PBC accept ownership regarding the issue.

- The coach does not own the problem, and it must remain that way through the end of the coaching conversation.

- The PBC must own the situation, problem, or request and be responsible and accountable for making the agreed-on changes or progress.

- Avoid use of the word "we" and use "you" instead (e.g., "What can you do. . . ?").

Assess the Gap (Current Reality to the Ideal State)

- It is helpful to have an idea of what the gap is.

- The PBC should be able to identify "I'm here" (current reality) and I need or want to get to "here (ideal state)," whatever "here" means to the PBC.

Discover

DISCOVER IS THE HEART OF THE COACHING CONVERSATION

Most of your time in the Discover stage will be spent working on two goals:

Discover Root Causes

- Many issues are not what they seem. Discovering root causes often requires that you probe more deeply into the depths of the situation. You can do this by remaining focused on the PBC and staying in tune to what is and is not being said.

- Refrain from jumping to conclusions. Instead, use a more scientific method. Make a hypothesis that you will test by asking probing and open-ended coaching questions.

- Look for themes or patterns of behavior at a high level. Do this without getting too caught up in the detail of the story. It may not be about what is said as much as what is really happening under the surface at an emotional or behavioral level.

Explore Alternatives

- Successful coaching results when PBCs explore alternatives, generate ideas, and discover solutions for themselves.

- Not solving for the PBC seems to be the hardest shift in thinking for coaches to master. Once you have mastered it, you will experience the true power of coaching.

Commit

Stage III, Commit, is about the PBC reaching a new level of commitment. You will focus on three goals to achieve this.

The general and overarching goal of coaching is to achieve commitment to sustained superior performance while maintaining positive work relationships. The Commit stage helps accomplish this.

Create an Action Plan

- The PBC should identify what steps or course of action is required to move forward and solve the issues discussed.

- Creating an action plan can take a number of different forms and do not always need to be in writing.

- Action plans can focus on the first step or any step that the PBC is planning to take. They can be more conceptual action steps over a period of time.

- Action steps do not have to be sequential.

What makes a good action plan?

- All plans should include concrete, observable actions and behaviors that do more than convey vague intentions.

- Plans include a built-in means of measuring future progress and success.

- The PBC should believe in, be energized by, and committed to the plan.

- The PBC assumes all responsibility for the plan. Your role is to support the PBC's progress and actions.

Eliminate Roadblocks and Obstacles

- Have the PBC identify roadblocks, potential obstacles, risks, and how to overcome them.

- This increases the level of commitment to the PBC's chosen course of action and his or her confidence to follow through with the plan.

Recap

Even if time is limited, do not skip the recap!

- Recap is the process of completing and summarizing the coaching conversation.
- The PBC (not the coach) provides a recap of the learning or major takeaways from the coaching conversation.
- Recap builds a sense of completeness and closure.
- The coach provides an encouraging reply that validates the PBC's progress, plan, and/or learnings.
- Coach or PBC confirms follow-up steps: next meeting or progress check. The PBC should drive the follow-up, not the coach.
- Closure occurs when people feel that they have experienced an *ah-ha* moment or learned something.

Recap Ideas

What kinds of things can you say to get the PBC to do the recap of the conversation (instead of you)?

_____

_____

_____

_____

_____

_____

_____

_____

_____

> The goal of the Commit stage is to reinforce the PBC's sense of achievement and ultimately obtain what you were striving for:
>
> **"Coaching for Commitment"**

Remember: Coaching is a tool for improving performance and enhancing esteem.

Coaching Demonstration

Demonstration Activity

Watch the coaching demonstration and try to determine when the coach transitions from one stage to the next and which goals are met.

Trust

❑ Coach established comfort and trust.

InDiCom Coaching Model

Stage I: Involve

❑ Purpose and expectations were clear.

❑ Ownership was established.

❑ Assess the gap (current to ideal—I'm "here" and I want to be "here").

Stage II: Discover

❑ Root causes were discovered.

❑ Alternatives explored by the PBC.

Stage III: Commit

❑ PBC created an action plan.

❑ Roadblocks and obstacles were eliminated.

❑ PBC provided the recap.

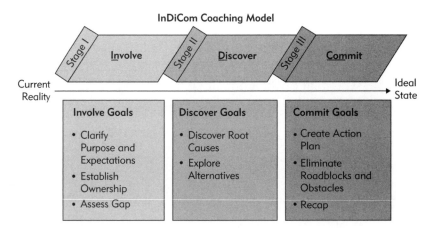

Coaching Circle

Participate in the coaching conversation. Determine when the conversation transitioned from one stage to the next and which goals are met.

Trust

☐ Coach established comfort and trust.

InDiCom Coaching Model

Stage I: Involve

☐ Purpose and expectations were clear.

☐ Ownership was established.

☐ Gap assessed (current to ideal—I'm "here" and I want to be "here").

Stage II: Discover

☐ Root causes were discovered.

☐ Alternatives explored by the PBC.

Stage III: Commit

☐ PBC created an action plan.

☐ Roadblocks and obstacles were eliminated.

☐ PBC provided the recap.

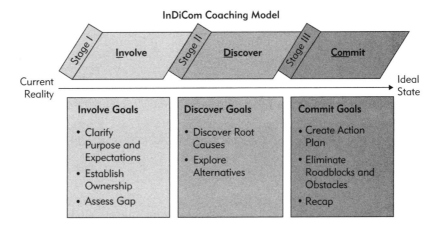

Coaching Circle

Participate in the coaching conversation. Determine when the conversation transitioned from one stage to the next and which goals are met.

Trust

❑ Coach established comfort and trust.

InDiCom Coaching Model

Stage I: Involve

❑ Purpose and expectations were clear.

❑ Ownership was established.

❑ Gap assessed (current to ideal—I'm "here" and I want to be "here").

Stage II: Discover

❑ Root causes were discovered.

❑ Alternatives explored by the PBC.

Stage III: Commit

❑ PBC created an action plan.

❑ Roadblocks and obstacles were eliminated.

❑ PBC provided the recap.

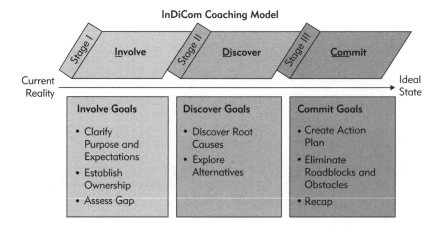

Coaching Circle

Participate in the coaching conversation. Determine when the conversation transitioned from one stage to the next and which goals were met.

Trust

    ❑ Coach established comfort and trust.

InDiCom Coaching Model

Stage I: Involve

    ❑ Purpose and expectations were clear.

    ❑ Ownership was established.

    ❑ Gap assessed (current to ideal—I'm "here" and I want to be "here").

Stage II: Discover

    ❑ Root causes were discovered.

    ❑ Alternatives explored by the PBC.

Stage III: Commit

    ❑ PBC created an action plan.

    ❑ Roadblocks and obstacles were eliminated.

    ❑ PBC provided the RECAP.

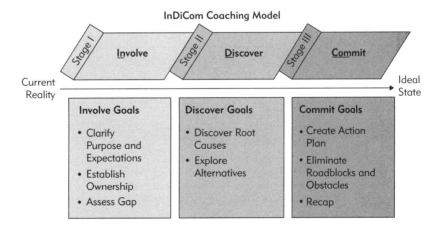

Video Coaching Scenarios

COACHING SCENARIO 1

Evaluate the **coach** according to the InDiCom coaching model.

Involve:

What was the purpose of the coaching conversation?

Who owned the issue? Coach or PBC (circle one)

Discover:

Who generated the solutions? Coach or PBC (circle one)

Commit:

Was an action plan established? Yes or No (circle one)

Who provided the recap? Coach or PBC (circle one)

Overall

What did the coach do well?

How could the coach improve?

COACHING SCENARIO 2

Evaluate the **coach** according to the InDiCom coaching model.

Involve:

How long did it take for the real problem to be identified?

Who owned the issue? Coach or PBC (circle one)

Discover:

Who generated the solutions? Coach or PBC (circle one)

Commit:

Was an action plan established? Yes or No (circle one)

If yes, whose solution was used? Coach or PBC (circle one)

Were roadblocks and obstacles eliminated? Yes or No (circle one)

Who provided the recap? Coach or PBC (circle one)

Overall

What did the coach do well?

How could the coach improve?

COACHING SCENARIO 3

Evaluate the **coach** according to the InDiCom coaching model.

This is an example of a performance coaching conversation. Watch how the coach presents the purpose (WHY), with an impact statement, and then wants the PBC to determine WHAT the real issue is.

Involve:

Who owned the REAL issue? Coach or PBC (circle one)

Discover:

Who generated the solutions? Coach or PBC (circle one)

Commit:

Was an action plan established? Yes or No (circle one)

If yes, whose solution was used? Coach or PBC (circle one)

Who provided the recap? Coach or PBC (circle one)

Overall

What did the coach do well?

How could the coach improve?

COACHING SCENARIO 4

Evaluate the **coach** according to the InDiCom coaching model.

This is an example of a team coaching conversation. Watch how the team leader presents "WHY" they are all there, and how they never really discover WHAT the issue is. No matter how much problem solving they do, they continue to guess about the core issue and the root cause.

Involve:

What did the team leader do that modeled good coaching behaviors?

Did the team ever establish complete ownership and agreement?

Discover:

Were the solutions they were exploring workable? Yes or No (circle one)

Commit:

Who provided the recap and follow-up statements? Leader or Team (circle one)

Overall

What did the team do well, in terms of using a coach approach?

How could the team improve, in terms of using a coach approach?

Who was in the coach role most often? Leader or Team Member (circle one)

My Turn

What one tool or skill will I take away from this module?

_____

_____

_____

_____

_____

_____

_____

_____

_____

_____

_____

_____

_____

_____

_____

Homework:

- Conduct a coaching conversation with someone tonight.
- Practice using the InDiCom coaching model.

6

CLEAR Coaching Skills

 3 hours, 35 minutes

Total Recall

Module 6 Objectives

In this module, you will have the opportunity to. . .

- **Become involved** with each of the CLEAR coaching skills.
- **Discover** your coaching skill gap.
- **Commit** to using the CLEAR coaching skills through practice, practice, practice.

There are times when you don't know what you are listening for—and that's okay.

Difficult Decisions

Think of a difficult decision that you are facing right now or know that you will have to make in the future.

Using CLEAR Coaching Skills

C hallenge

L isten

E ncourage

A sk

R efine

Although many of the coaching skills that you learn may be familiar to you, because you use them in everyday conversations, you will learn how to apply these common communication skills from a *coach role* to achieve maximum impact in a coaching conversation and to be conscious of your use of them.

CSI—My Coaching Skills Gap

Refer back to the CSI to find your Coaching Skills Gap.

The skill I need to work on the most, according to the CSI, is?
Check the skill(s) with the lowest score.

- ❑ **C** hallenge
- ❑ **L** isten
- ❑ **E** ncourage
- ❑ **A** sk
- ❑ **R** efine

Challenge

Challenge is about helping the PBC experience an *ah-ha* moment. It is used when the PBC is stuck and needs a little push or when the PBC requires feedback regarding incongruence between behaviors or comments. The purpose of Challenge is to provide the PBC with insight that will help move him or her forward, either in discovering the root cause, moving toward his or her ideal, creating a plan of action, or moving away from an impending disaster.

Techniques to use to Challenge the PBC:

REQUEST

Request is about encouraging PBCs to take risks and challenging them to stretch out of their comfort zones in order to learn a new skill, understand what it's like to be in someone else's shoes, eliminate or face fears, etc. Requests Challenge the status quo of the PBC.

Never make a request as a means of getting your (hidden) agenda met.

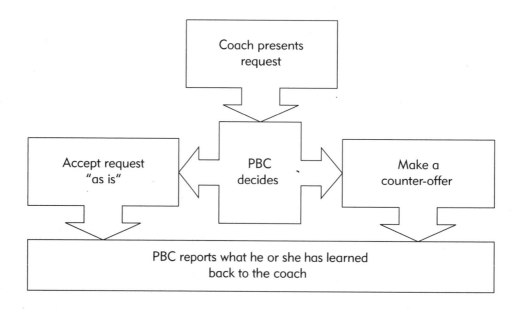

I Challenge you to. . .

_____

_____

_____

_____

_____

_____

_____

Requests

- If the PBC cannot manage to get through a team meeting without correcting a colleague or direct report, it may be appropriate to Challenge him or her to not speak at all during the next meeting.

- If the PBC consistently tells (fixes) versus asks when in the *coach role* with others, it could be useful for the person to try only asking questions for an entire day (at home as well as at work).

- If the PBC has a personality conflict with a peer, it may be appropriate to request that he or she take that person out to lunch or for coffee with a goal of finding a common interest.

- If the PBC is someone who feels as though he or she doesn't get enough recognition from his or her manager, encourage the PBC to model what he or she wants by finding a reason to compliment the boss, first!

- If the PBC aspires to become a project manager but has never tried complex project management, try requesting that he or she take on a small, simple project to test his or her skills and ability (PBC chooses project).

- If a PBC has a fear of failure or is a perfectionist, it may be appropriate to Challenge or request that he or she fail at something, anything, during the next week. This doesn't have to be big or reckless.

- If the PBC is struggling with diversity issues, it might be worthwhile to make a request that he or she do some volunteering at an organization that embodies what he or she does not understand. (Some companies give employees recognition or credit for charity work.)

- If the PBC is struggling with rejection or not being included, make a request that the PBC try to get ten rejections within one week or day. He or she may find it is harder to be rejected than originally thought!

REALITY CHECK

There are times when coaches can and should serve as a resource for removing blind spots and be someone who provides hard-hitting feedback to the PBC. This is called a **Reality Check**.

A reality check is a short, succinct statement, not a question, that addresses the issue.

Use a reality check when you:

- See or hear a critical disconnect in what the PBC is saying versus doing.

- See a blind spot that the PBC refuses to see or acknowledge.

- Identify a recurring pattern of behavior.

- Experience your intuition kicking in, saying, "Pay attention; something is going on here." Then address it.

- Want to make an attempt to call the PBC on his or her actions or behavior.

How should a Reality Check be delivered?

- You should make one attempt to call the PBC on the disconnect, using a short, succinct statement.

- It is not necessary to put the Reality Check the form of a question.

- Speak the truth, while maintaining esteem and trust.

"Say what you mean but don't say it mean. How the other person takes it is up to him or her."

WHAT DOES A REALITY CHECK SOUND LIKE?

"You keep telling me that you trust your employees, but your micro-management says you don't.

"It's not surprising that you don't reward or recognize your employees, since you don't require recognition yourself."

"You are taking on so much responsibility for your team's success; you are actually doing more harm than good."

"You cannot save everyone from feeling the pain of the upcoming changes."

"It appears you are playing the role of mother to your employees more than the role of leader."

"You are operating out of fear."

"It appears you are more concerned with seeking approval than with leading."

What If I'm Wrong?

The PBC will immediately say, "No, that's not it." You should not try to force your perspective on the PBC, but should return to where you left off.

What If I'm Right?

When you nail the issue on the head, the PBC will usually remain silent for a moment (allow this silence to happen), or may affirm your comment. The results are dramatic, as the PBC has just experienced an *a-ha* moment that will have a lasting shift in his or her way of thinking and/or behaviors.

INTUITION

Intuition is part of the Challenge skill because you use it to tell you when to deliver a reality check or request.

Think of *intuition* like an alarm clock. The clock goes off and you have two choices: wake up or hit the snooze button; address it or ignore it. By choosing to address it, you are making the choice to take action. In coaching, when your *intuition* goes off, you can choose to make the coaching conversation more productive by addressing what your *intuition* is telling you. *Intuition* helps you discover root causes to issues that would normally go undiscovered or be dealt with at a surface level. Next time your *intuition* goes off, *wake up*!

 One caution about the use of intuition: Be willing to be wrong!

Where does your intuition come from? (check one)

_____ A little voice inside your head

_____ A racing heart

_____ A feeling in the pit of your stomach that acts as a sixth sense

_____ Other (explain)

Use intuition to know when to deliver requests or reality checks!

Listen

Listen is about being psychologically committed to the conversation.

Think of Listen as a workout for the brain! The average person speaks at a rate of 125 to 175 words per minute, yet we can listen at a rate of 450 words per minute (Carver, Johnson, & Friedman, 1970), and we think at 1,000 to 3,000 words per minute (HighGain, 2000). So what fills the space between what is being said by the PBC and what is heard by the coach? Are you thinking of your next question? Formulating solutions? Creating a to-do list? Preparing an agenda for your next meeting? Putting together your shopping list? Or . . . Geez! What *is* that annoying noise down the hall?

As a coach, strive to become an exceptional listener!

LISTEN

Listen requires the coach to be diligent in talking less and paying close attention to non-verbal clues. Listen simply means that the coach is listening for what *is not* said as much as for what *is* said. Listen beyond the words.

Listen asks you to:

- Be present and focused on the PBC.
- Show respect in your own verbal and non-verbal dialog.
- Let the PBC know he or she is being heard and understood.
- Stop multitasking (turn off your monitor/computer/cell phone, forward your phone, and do not do email while virtual coaching).
- Not make assumptions.

STORY TELLING

Encourage and solicit stories from the PBC. People who tell stories are more apt to reveal information that they may not normally share and, in many cases, a good coach (who is mentally present during the coaching conversation) can ascertain useful information from what is being said. Story telling can help the coach to better understand context, gaps, and the PBC's values, strengths, and needs, as well as what is going on under the surface. *Story telling* is a great way of engaging a listener—in this case, you. People learn through stories.

 As a coach be very careful when telling your own stories or providing self-disclosure. Not because there is a risk of sharing too much of yourself, but because there is a risk of not knowing when enough is enough! Be careful not to take over the conversation.

What can you say to get people to share their stories?

- "That sounds interesting. Tell me more."
- "What can you share?"
- "What's going on?"
- "I'd like to hear what you think."
- "What are your concerns?"
- "What are you struggling with?"
- "Is there something more that you would like to share?"
- "Tell me about your house, kids, pets, job. . ." (Whatever the person mentioned as a natural part of the conversation)
- "Wow! That sounds like a great story. I'd love to hear it."

_____

_____

_____

_____

_____

_____

_____

_____

_____

_____

BENEFITS OF SILENCE

Learn how to embrace silence.

Silence can be a very useful tool, especially in the world of coaching. Learning to use silence effectively benefits both coach and the PBC because it creates space in the conversation for processing and reflection.

If you struggle with silence, count: 1, 2, 3, 4. . . for however long it takes when the PBC needs process time!

Ideally, learn to quiet your mind and just wait.

Don't feel the need to fill the space when there is silence.

Shhhhhhh. . . . . .

"Silence Is Golden!"

Encourage

Encourage is all about making PBCs feel good, validating their feelings and emotions, and recognizing their accomplishments. This gives them reason to continue moving forward toward success. It is an essential part of coaching because it enhances esteem and confidence.

The Encourage skill builds on other skills by making the coaching conversation personal and individualized. The coach provides validation statements that recognize and acknowledge the PBC's feelings and emotions in the coaching conversation.

As much as the coach plays the role of truthsayer, reality-check person, and occasionally devil's advocate, the coach is also the PBC's biggest cheerleader and supporter!

As part of building trust before, and maintaining it throughout the coaching conversation, recognize and reward PBCs for their insights, efforts, and accomplishments. This can be done through the use of the Encourage skill.

VALIDATE FEELINGS AND EMOTIONS

Validate means that you address, acknowledge, and bring to light the emotion or feeling that is being conveyed by the PBC. This alone will help PBCs discover root causes to their situation faster than anything else you can do.

If the PBC uses any of the following words in your coaching conversation take pause, address and discuss the feelings. This is only a partial list and it doesn't matter where or how these words are used, or in what context within the coaching conversation. The point is to listen for the feelings and either acknowledge or ask about them. Remember, *positive* feelings and emotions should be acknowledged, too.

Thrilled	Annoyed	Stressed
Afraid	Angry	Anxious
Amazed	Frustrated	Worried
Excited	Confused	Relieved
Hate	Surprised	Hopeful
Concerned	Confident	Trust/Don't trust
Disappointed	Believe	Feel
Don't care		

How can you do this?

With validation statements such as:

- "You sound angry. What is making you angry?"
- "You sound stressed. Where is the stress coming from?"
- "I can hear the frustration in your voice. Where is it coming from?"
- "You're not quite yourself today. Would you like to talk?"
- "I can tell that this confusion is really bothering you."
- "You mentioned that you're disappointed, tell me more."
- "You seem re-energized already."

Create Your Own. . .

Think of an emotion or feeling. If you were to hear this emotion or feeling (in word or tone) in your coaching conversation, what could you say to acknowledge or validate it?

_____

_____

_____

_____

_____

_____

_____

_____

Which emotion or feeling is the most difficult for you to deal with?

_____

_____

_____

_____

_____

_____

_____

_____

_____

CELEBRATE!

Celebrate is another way to Encourage PBCs and should be ongoing throughout the coaching conversation. *Celebrate* by recognizing the PBC. The misconception is that celebration has to be some type of ticker-tape parade that announces stellar performance to the world or a gushing display of gratitude. Not true. It can be as simple as a "Thank you for a job well done," "I'm proud of you," or "You did a lot of work here."

Celebrate **Big** and Small Accomplishments!

Celebration Statements

"Congratulations on letting your team members run the meeting!"

"This is a personal success for you!"

"Your ability to engage others is quite good; it made a big impact in today's meeting because you made everyone feel heard."

"What you just said/did was huge. Do you realize that?"

"How can you celebrate the fact that you have accomplished . . . ?"

"Let's take a moment to discuss how much you have accomplished here."

"WOW! You have made great progress!"

What celebration statements can *you* think of?

_____

_____

_____

_____

_____

_____

_____

_____

_____

_____

_____

_____

Ask

COACHING QUESTIONS

Ask is about asking probing, thought-provoking, discovery-oriented, compelling, and pivotal questions.

Coaching questions are those that make the PBC think. They are searching and open-ended and do not restrict the respondent to one- or two-word answers; nor do they restrict by implying opinions or biases of the coach. Coaching questions allow people to process information verbally and make connections. They allow great latitude for the PBC to discover how to achieve the ideal state.

Guidelines for Using the Ask Skill

- Remain *egoless*

- Pretend you weren't the expert.

- Be aware of your tone.

- Only ask if you are willing to hear the answer (his or hers).

- Use care in making statements that impose a bias.

- If you are unclear, ask more questions.

- Questions should not take the place of statements. If you have something to say, say it!

- Allow the PBC to answer questions without interrupting.

- Avoid questions that lead the PBC in one direction or the other: "Have you thought of. . .?" "Did you try. . .?" "Would it be helpful for you to. . .?" These kinds of questions communicate that there is a right and wrong way to do something and the right way is your way.

- When it comes to legal or compliance issues, don't ask unless there is room for flexibility and autonomy.

Goal: Find out information! Ask! Don't tell!

Tips for Creating Great Coaching Questions

- There are no perfect questions. If you remain objective, the right questions will come to you at the right time.

- It is not imperative that you think of a question immediately after the PBC stops talking. You can have process time.

- "What" and "how" questions are the most impactful, are compelling, and draw out the most information from PBCs. "What" questions diagnose and solve. "How" questions give clarity and are great for determining specific actions. Ask questions that start with "What" and "how."

  - What have you tried?

  - How do you know?

  - What is the ideal?

  - How can you make this happen?

- "Why" questions should be limited to avoid placing blame or encountering defensiveness. "Why" questions can be appropriate only if you ensure they do not imply blame or put the PBC on the defensive. Sometimes adding a phrase before the why can be helpful. (Be careful of your tone when using these.)

  - Do you understand why you are hesitating?

  - Or turn a "why" question into a "what" question: "What are you hesitating about?"

- Keep questions short, succinct, and clear.

- Ask one question at a time. Do not rapid fire several questions at once.

POWERFUL STATEMENTS

Powerful statements are **not** the same as reality checks **or** requests.

They are statements used in place of a coaching question. They are what you use to keep the coaching conversation going.

Powerful statements are those brief verbal responses that communicate to the PBC that you are fully present and that you are involved in the conversation. We sometimes refer to this as "verbal nodding."

Powerful statements and verbal nodding create an environment for PBCs to continue talking and to expand on what they are saying.

As Simple As. . .

"Tell me more about that."

"Really." (Pause)

"Let's hear the latest."

"I've gotten conflicting reports." (Pause)

"I've heard good things." (Pause)

"Sounds like a story." (Pause)

"I'm listening." (Careful with tone on this one!)

"Go on."

"Please continue."

"Uh huh."

"mmmm."

"I see."

"O.K."

"Yes."

"Right."

"I understand."

"Yes, I follow that."

"Oh yes, I see where you are going."

THIRTY-FIVE GREAT COACHING QUESTIONS

1. How are things going?
2. How are you going to make that happen?
3. How can you be genuine/authentic in your response?
4. How can you influence this?
5. How do you feel about that?
6. How do you get the best out of people?
7. How do you let them know?
8. How has that gotten in your way?
9. How is that working for you?
10. How is this messing with your values? (Or rephrase the question and name the value.)
11. Tell me about your role model(s)? (Tie into changing behaviors.)
12. Tell me more.
13. What advice would you give someone in your shoes?
14. What are you afraid of?
15. What are you dependent on?
16. What assumptions are you making?
17. What does the ideal look like?
18. What is draining you/your team?
19. What is the best you can hope for?
20. What is the cost of that action/inaction/behavior?
21. What is the first thing you are going to do?
22. What is the worst question I could ask you right now?
23. What makes you say/think that?
24. What one word describes where you are at now? (Ask with Question 25.)
25. What one word describes your ideal?
26. What should you be modeling?
27. What should you be paying attention to?
28. What should your role be?
29. What three words do you want people to use when describing you? (Ask with Question 30.)

(continued)

30. What do you need to do to live those three words?

31. What would you do if you did know? (Use when PBC responds with "I don't know.")

32. What would you do if there were no rules? (You can negotiate from here.)

33. What would you like to talk about?

34. What would your best friend/someone you admire tell you to do?

35. What is the underlying emotion you are feeling?

Refine

The Refine skill keeps the conversation on track and relevant.

The Refine skill is about making sure that the coaching conversation is primarily unidirectional in nature. That is not to say that the dialog won't have its twists, turns, and even backward glances, but ultimately that is will move the PBC forward to action.

What gets a conversation off-track?

The PBC may:

_____ others for their circumstances.

Have strong emotional _____ (anger, fear, anxiety).

_____ _____: make little or no verbal response.

Begin to cover the same _____ over and over again.

Be _____ by the _____ and need time to prepare to discuss it.

Become too tired or distracted to further the _____ .

_____ so long it becomes counter-productive.

_____ on about irrelevant _____ .

_____ —intentionally or unintentionally!

Word Bank

blame	shut down	outbursts	ramble	dodge
things	surprised	topic	ground	topic
conversation	vent	conversation		

How do you refocus a conversation when it goes off track?

_____

_____

_____

_____

Be reasonable in your redirection and allow for some digression and discussion that is off topic. Simply be wary of when refining is needed, but use it when it is.

REFINE SAMPLES

- Redirect by validating concerns/feelings without allowing the divergent topic to take over the conversation. Then restate the goal or the objective:

  ○ "Wendy, I can see that discussing your success is making you uncomfortable. We all need recognition from time to time, and I can assure you that this is not a way of getting you to do more work. I simply think you are ready for the next level if you want to go there."

- Politely stop the divergent conversation and redirect to the specific outcomes you have agreed on or reiterate the ideal state:

  ○ "Excuse me, Dawn, I can appreciate that you have a complex life outside of work. As your coach, I am concerned about your life here at work. How can you focus on you and your sales numbers right now?"

- Ask the PBC to focus on the solution, not on the problem:

  ○ "Beth, you are not being blamed or criticized. I simply need your help in solving this issue so that there is a positive outcome for everyone."

- Ask PBCs to focus on themselves, their part, their responsibility (and not that of others):

  ○ "I appreciate your input and understand your feelings. Right now we are talking about you. It's my job to worry about everyone else on the team. How can you improve your partnering skills?"

- Find out what the PBC has influence (if not control) over in the situation:

  ○ "What partners or pieces of the project can you influence, Heidi?"

- Explore what the PBC can own:

  ○ "What three things can you commit to at this time?"

- Reassure PBCs that you have their best interests at heart and that your *role is to help them:*

  ○ "I want to assure you that I am interested in your success and part of my role as your coach is to point out any obstacles that might impede that success."

- Call out the behavior or the (suspected) emotion and ask where the person being coached would like to go from there:

  ○ "What are you avoiding? (pause for response) What would you like to do about it?"

TWO-WORDS

Two-Words is a way of helping PBCs gain clarity about the gap by identifying current reality versus the ideal state they are trying to reach. To use *Two-Words,* ask the following two coaching questions in succession:

Current Reality: "What **one word** best describes where you are, right now, with your situation?" Allow PBCs to come up with their own words (words or phrases are okay, too).

Ideal State: "Now, what **one word** would best describes what you want it to be, your ideal?" Allow the PBC to answer.

Putting the Two-Words together, in a "From/To" format helps identify the gap.

The Power of Two Little Words

Fill in the blank with possible answers the PBC might provide. The first two are completed for you. Be prepared to share.

Outcast **to** accepted

Driven **to** effective

Tired **to** _____

_____ **to** coach

Authoritative **to** _____

Fearful **to** _____

_____ **to** purposeful

Sledge hammer **to** _____

Aggressive **to** _____

Challenged **to** _____

_____ **to** freedom

Caretaker **to** _____

METAPHORS

Metaphors. . .

- Are a figure of speech, symbol, or image that can help illustrate a point and connect seemingly dissimilar things.

- Are an effective way to put a situation or issue into a context so the PBC can better understand it.

- Are a way to connect images or descriptions of everyday things, previous experiences, or applications of prior knowledge with the present situation.

- Allow PBCs to relate their current situations to something that they already have expertise or knowledge around so that they can move forward.

My Difficult Decision Is/Was. . .

_____

_____

_____

_____

_____

The Power of Metaphors

When people are able to see how to apply familiar processes and behaviors or attach their situations to something they know inside and out, it makes it easier for them to come up with action plans. It also enhances esteem and gives them confidence. Using metaphors can be a tremendous tool for moving PBCs forward. Typically, PBCs know they need to do something, they just don't know where to start. Some common metaphors that can be used in coaching are:

- Sports
- Scrapbooking
- Parenting
- Objects ("I am a ship adrift at sea.")
- Learning to driving a car
- TV/movies
- Spiritual/Religious

To use a metaphor, simply listen for clues such as being involved in sports or having children, and see whether a PBC's knowledge in one area can be transferred over to the coaching topic.

Metaphor How To's

As the coach, you are welcome to help PBCs come up with metaphors. If you really want to challenge yourself as a coach, learn how to have PBCs come up with their own metaphors!

If you know the PBC's interests, hobbies, etc., you can help identify a metaphor:

- "How is this similar to you not being able to be on the football field, playing the game for your kids?"
- "How is this similar to putting together a 5,000 piece jigsaw puzzle?" (Build the frame first, then complete the large center point object, then work on the detail.)

Encourage the PBC to come up with the metaphor.

- "Is there anything else in your life that you can compare this to?"
- "When have you been in a similar situation?"
- "When have you felt this way before?"
- "Is there a way for you to connect this to something you already know, are good at, etc. . . . ."
- "Is there any other challenging time in your life that you came through well?"

Once metaphors have been identified and explored, encourage PBCs to share how their current situations relate to the metaphor.

WHAT YOU SHOULD KNOW ABOUT CLEAR. . .

- CLEAR coaching skills are used with all phases of the InDiCom coaching model.

- CLEAR coaching skills are common everyday communication skills that, when used from a coach's perspective, are designed to achieve maximum impact in a coaching conversation.

- Integrating CLEAR coaching skills into your skill set takes sustained effort, time, and practice!

TIME TO PRACTICE!

Practice, Practice, Practice = Coach

Coaching Circle

Actively participate in the coaching conversation by practicing your CLEAR coaching skills. Use this checklist to capture skills covered. Skills may be covered in no particular order and some may not be covered at all.

	NOTES:
Challenge	
❑ Coach made request of PBC.	
❑ Coach provided a reality check.	
❑ Coach used intuition.	
Listen	
❑ Coach listened intently.	
❑ Coach used silence.	
❑ Coach didn't interrupt or over-talk.	
❑ Coach encouraged story telling.	
❑ Coach limited self-disclosure.	
Encourage	
❑ Coach acknowledged feelings and emotions.	
❑ Coach encouraged the PBC.	
❑ Coach used validate and celebrate statements.	
Ask	
❑ Coach asked thought-provoking and open-ended coaching questions.	
❑ Coach did not use rapid-fire questions.	
❑ Coach kept questions simple.	
Refine	
❑ Coach kept the conversation and the PBC on track and focused.	
❑ Coach helped PBC to take accountability.	
❑ Coach tried Two-Words.	
❑ Coach tried using metaphors.	

Practice, Practice, Practice = Coach

Coaching Circle

Actively participate in the coaching conversation by practicing your CLEAR coaching skills. Use this checklist to capture skills covered. Skills may be covered in no particular order and some may not be covered at all.

	NOTES:
Challenge	
❏ Coach made request of PBC.	
❏ Coach provided a reality check.	
❏ Coach used intuition.	
Listen	
❏ Coach listened intently.	
❏ Coach used silence.	
❏ Coach didn't interrupt or over-talk.	
❏ Coach encouraged story telling.	
❏ Coach limited self-disclosure.	
Encourage	
❏ Coach acknowledged feelings and emotions.	
❏ Coach encouraged the PBC.	
❏ Coach used validate and celebrate statements.	
Ask	
❏ Coach asked thought-provoking and open-ended coaching questions.	
❏ Coach did not use rapid-fire questions.	
❏ Coach kept questions simple.	
Refine	
❏ Coach kept the conversation and the PBC on track and focused.	
❏ Coach helped PBC to take accountability.	
❏ Coach tried Two-Words.	
❏ Coach tried using metaphors.	

Practice, Practice, Practice = Coach

Coaching Circle

Actively participate in the coaching conversation by practicing your CLEAR coaching skills. Use this checklist to capture skills covered. Skills may be covered in no particular order and some may not be covered at all.

	NOTES:
Challenge ❏ Coach made request of PBC. ❏ Coach provided a reality check. ❏ Coach used intuition. **Listen** ❏ Coach listened intently. ❏ Coach used silence. ❏ Coach didn't interrupt or over-talk. ❏ Coach encouraged story telling. ❏ Coach limited self-disclosure. **Encourage** ❏ Coach acknowledged feelings and emotions. ❏ Coach encouraged the PBC. ❏ Coach used validate and celebrate statements. **Ask** ❏ Coach asked thought-provoking and open-ended coaching questions. ❏ Coach did not use rapid-fire questions. ❏ Coach kept questions simple. **Refine** ❏ Coach kept the conversation and the PBC on track and focused. ❏ Coach helped PBC to take accountability. ❏ Coach tried Two-Words. ❏ Coach tried using metaphors.	

Practice, Practice, Practice = Coach

Coaching Circle

Actively participate in the coaching conversation by practicing your CLEAR coaching skills. Use this checklist to capture skills covered. Skills may be covered in no particular order and some may not be covered at all.

Challenge

- ❑ Coach made request of PBC.
- ❑ Coach provided a reality check.
- ❑ Coach used intuition.

Listen

- ❑ Coach listened intently.
- ❑ Coach used silence.
- ❑ Coach didn't interrupt or over-talk.
- ❑ Coach encouraged story telling.
- ❑ Coach limited self-disclosure.

Encourage

- ❑ Coach acknowledged feelings and emotions.
- ❑ Coach encouraged the PBC.
- ❑ Coach used validate and celebrate statements.

Ask

- ❑ Coach asked thought-provoking and open-ended coaching questions.
- ❑ Coach did not use rapid-fire questions.
- ❑ Coach kept questions simple.

Refine

- ❑ Coach kept the conversation and the PBC on track and focused.
- ❑ Coach helped PBC to take accountability.
- ❑ Coach tried Two-Words.
- ❑ Coach tried using metaphors.

NOTES:

My Turn

My biggest learning from this module was . . .

_____

_____

_____

_____

_____

_____

_____

_____

_____

_____

_____

_____

_____

_____

_____

_____

_____

_____

_____

_____

_____

_____

Plan to Coach

 2 hours, 40 minutes

Module 7 Objectives

In this module, you will have the opportunity to. . .

- **Get involved** by conducting a live coaching session.
- **Discover** how it all comes together into a successful coaching conversation.
- **Commit** to being the coach.

Ignoring problems does not make them go away!

Plan to Coach

It's time for you to plan for your practice coaching session. There are two things you need to plan for:

- Being the PBC.
- Being the coach.

My Role as the PBC

You will bring a real live coaching topic to the table. Think of a current leadership challenge, a personal development area, or something you are struggling with. Take a moment to write down the key issues you would like to receive coaching on—no third-party scenarios or coach-the-coach situations. This is your situation and you will be receiving coaching for you!

_____

_____

_____

_____

_____

_____

My Role as the Coach

Be prepared to put your coaching hat on! Remember, don't worry about asking perfect questions, *Listen* first, then *Ask* the best questions you have at the right times.

Things I want to remember about the InDiCom coaching model and stage goals.

_____

_____

_____

Coaching skills I want to practice or focus on.

_____

_____

_____

Coach's Notes

Use this as your guide for conducting your coaching conversations and capturing notes.

Name (PBC):   **Coach:**   **Date:**

Shift to Coach Role!				

<table>
<tr><td rowspan="3" style="writing-mode:vertical">InDiCom Coaching Model</td><td colspan="5">

INVOLVE

Purpose and Expectations
PBC accepted ownership
Identified gap

DISCOVER

Root causes (core issues)
PBC's ideas and solutions

COMMIT

PBC's plan of action
Roadblocks/obstacles discussed
PBC's recap
Follow-up plans

</td></tr>
</table>

	CHALLENGE	**LISTEN**	**ENCOURAGE**	**ASK**	**REFINE**
CLEAR	Request Reality Check	Story Telling Benefits of Silence	Validate Celebrate	Coaching Questions Powerful Statements	Two-Words Metaphors

Notes for Next Meeting

Remember to ask about during the next session:

Key areas PBC is working on:

COACH EVALUATION

Observer: Rate the skills of the coach, not the topic of the coaching conversation. Using the scale below, rate the extent to which the coach demonstrated the behavior indicated. Be objective in your evaluation and capture examples where possible

5 = To a Great Extent	3 = Somewhat	1 = Not Really

InDiCom Coaching Model	Rating
Coach was attentive to the needs of the PBC?	5 4 3 2 1
Coach focused on clarifying the purpose?	5 4 3 2 1
Coach kept the ownership of the situation on the PBC?	5 4 3 2 1
Gap was identified?	5 4 3 2 1
Coach allowed autonomy and innovation in generating solutions?	5 4 3 2 1
Coach resisted fixing the problem/situation for the PBC?	5 4 3 2 1
Coach facilitated the PBC's creation of an action plan?	5 4 3 2 1
Coach discussed barriers and obstacles?	5 4 3 2 1
Coach had the PBC provide the recap?	5 4 3 2 1
The conversation felt natural.	5 4 3 2 1

CLEAR Coaching Skills	
Challenge: Coach used intuition to stay in tune with the PBC?	5 4 3 2 1

Bonus: Coach presented a *request* or *reality check?* Yes or No *(circle one)*

Listen: The coach heard and understood what was being said?	5 4 3 2 1
Encourage: Coach used validate and celebrate statements?	5 4 3 2 1
Ask: Coach asked coaching questions (did not lead or rapid-fire questions)?	5 4 3 2 1
Refine: Coach kept the conversation on track and focused on the PBC's accountabilities?	5 4 3 2 1

Bonus: Coach used Two-Words or metaphor? Yes or No *(circle one)*

Additional Comments (use back of page, if desired):

COACH EVALUATION

Observer: Rate the skills of the coach, not the topic of the coaching conversation. Using the scale below, rate the extent to which the coach demonstrated the behavior indicated. Be objective in your evaluation and capture examples where possible

5 = To a Great Extent	3 = Somewhat	1 = Not Really

InDiCom Coaching Model	Rating
Coach was attentive to the needs of the PBC?	5 4 3 2 1
Coach focused on clarifying the purpose?	5 4 3 2 1
Coach kept the ownership of the situation on the PBC?	5 4 3 2 1
Gap was identified?	5 4 3 2 1
Coach allowed autonomy and innovation in generating solutions?	5 4 3 2 1
Coach resisted fixing the problem/situation for the PBC?	5 4 3 2 1
Coach facilitated the PBC's creation of an action plan?	5 4 3 2 1
Coach discussed barriers and obstacles?	5 4 3 2 1
Coach had the PBC provide the recap?	5 4 3 2 1
The conversation felt natural.	5 4 3 2 1

CLEAR Coaching Skills	
Challenge: Coach used intuition to stay in tune with the PBC?	5 4 3 2 1
Bonus: Coach presented a *request* or *reality check? Yes or No (circle one)*	
Listen: The coach heard and understood what was being said?	5 4 3 2 1
Encourage: Coach used validate and celebrate statements?	5 4 3 2 1
Ask: Coach asked coaching questions (did not lead or rapid-fire questions)?	5 4 3 2 1
Refine: Coach kept the conversation on track and focused on the PBC's accountabilities?	5 4 3 2 1

Bonus: Coach used Two-Words or metaphor? Yes or No (circle one)

Additional Comments (use back of page, if desired):

Coach Learning Journal

As the coach, what did I do well?

_____

_____

_____

_____

_____

What did I learn about coaching from this experience?

_____

_____

_____

_____

_____

What surprised me (good or bad)?

_____

_____

_____

_____

_____

If I could do something over, what would it be?

_____

_____

_____

_____

_____

Performance Coaching

TIPS FOR CONDUCTING A PERFORMANCE COACHING CONVERSATION

- Be clear with the PBC about WHY the conversation is happening.

- Clarify purpose and expectations:
  - State objectives, outcomes, results, opportunities, and/or potential.
  - Precisely state the performance or proficiency area using specific examples, behaviors, results, or data.
  - Identify how the PBC's performance differs from your expectations or established standards.
  - Use a direct manner and include an impact statement that hits home with the PBC. ("When you are late, the team has to cover for you.")

- Avoid the laundry-list approach; issues should be dealt with one at a time.

- Start with the most recent example of the performance issue.

- PBC still owns it and must agree with you.

- Let go of the issue once it's been presented.

- Let the PBC determine WHAT needs to happen and HOW to make it happen.

- Avoid making assumptions that you know the cause of the problem.

- Be wary of starting out with a compliment that leads to a criticism.

- Avoid transition words such as "however," "but" and "on the other hand."

- Allow the PBC to talk, vent (if needed), explore, solve, and create an action plan.

- Be willing to accept incremental improvements that put ownership, and ultimately action, back onto the PBC.

- Have supporting facts, data, and numbers at the ready.

- Have key documents close by so you aren't searching for them during the conversation. This includes compliance policies, regulations, and any applicable training material.

Turning the issue over to the PBC may result in *you* seeing things differently, too. "What are you willing to accept?"

When you communicate the WHY, you accept the responsibility for managing the resistance that you create.

Reduce resistance and negative emotions by:

Know how to react when the PBC reacts.

Performance Coaching Worksheet

PBC: **Coach:**   **Date:**

Use this form to prepare for your performance coaching conversations, when you bring the *why* (*Why are we having this conversation?*) to the person being coached (PBC).

COACH'S OPENING. . .

Why is this conversation necessary? (Be specific.) How will I introduce it?

What does the PBC need to know about the situation and my expectations? (Most recent behavior versus expectations.)

What is the impact of the PBC's behavior on him or her, on me, the team, and/or the company?

How will I shift ownership so that the PBC owns the problem, gap, or issue? What question can I start with?

BEING FULLY PREPARED . . .

When and where will the coaching take place?

How will I eliminate distractions?

What will I say to establish and maintain trust?

How will I set the PBC at ease?

What is my ideal outcome? (If not ideal, what is the best I could hope for?)

How will I react if the PBC doesn't agree with my assessment?

If necessary, how will I depersonalize the situation?

What can I say to reduce resistance and/or remain focused on the future?

Are there things I need to own up to?/Was I unclear?/Is there an unusually heavy workload?/How can I communicate those things?

What positive feedback or acknowledgements will I use?

What is my timeline for visible progress?

What are my follow-up needs/commitments from the PBC?

What documents or data must be gathered before the meeting?

Additional Comments:

My Turn

My *ah-ha* from this module was. . .

_____

_____

_____

_____

_____

_____

_____

_____

_____

_____

_____

_____

_____

_____

_____

_____

_____

_____

_____

_____

_____

_____

_____

My Turn

8

Creating a Coaching for Commitment Culture

 30 minutes

Module 8 Objectives

In this module, you will have the opportunity to. . .

- **Become involved** by creating a value proposition for coaching.
- **Discover** how to implement the *coach role* into your world.
- **Commit** to creating a Coaching for Commitment Culture

. . .Knowing where you're going. . . priceless.

Steps to Create a Coaching for Commitment Culture

1. Use the InDiCom coaching model as your guide:

   <u>In</u>volve people.

   <u>Di</u>scover how coaching is currently used.

   <u>Com</u>mit to using a common coaching language.

2. Be an advocate for coaching being viewed as a positive interaction.

3. Teach the coaching concepts: model and skills.

4. Get the whole organization involved—top down. If organization-wide is out of the scope of possibility, start with your team.

5. Create a value proposition for coaching.

See the InDiCom Coaching Culture Guide on page 135 of this workbook. By completing the guide and answering the questions with your intact team, you will have addressed all five steps outlined above.

Create Your Value Proposition for Coaching

Use the statements below to assist you in creating your value proposition for coaching.

If I spend more time coaching, the *benefits to me* will be:

_____

_____

_____

_____

If I spend more time coaching, the benefits *to others* will be:

_____

_____

_____

_____

If I spend more time coaching, the benefits to *the organization* will be:

_____

_____

_____

_____

MY COACHING VALUE PROPOSITION

Using the examples on the slide and by combining the elements from the questions you answered above, create your own value proposition for coaching. Remember to include the benefits to you, your team, and the organization.

Why Coach? By Coaching. . .

_____

_____

_____

_____

Making Coaching Part of My Culture

Ideally, a Coaching for Commitment Culture starts at the top of an organization and trickles down. If that is not possible in your organization, then start with your team. Decide whether you will be thinking of your team or the organization before answering the following.

On a scale of 1 to 10, how well does Coaching for Commitment fit into my culture?

To a Great Extent   Not at All

10   9   8   7   6   5   4   3   2   1

What can I do to make coaching a greater part of my culture?

_____

_____

_____

_____

_____

_____

_____

_____

How will I apply what I learned here, with my team, in order to help foster a coaching culture?

_____

_____

_____

_____

_____

_____

_____

_____

How can I contribute to a coaching culture?

_____

_____

_____

_____

_____

_____

_____

_____

What obstacles might I encounter?

_____

_____

_____

_____

_____

_____

_____

_____

How will I overcome them?

_____

_____

_____

_____

_____

_____

_____

_____

_____

_____

_____

My Turn

What insight will I take away from this module?

_____

_____

_____

_____

_____

_____

_____

_____

_____

_____

_____

_____

_____

_____

_____

_____

_____

_____

_____

_____

_____

_____

_____

_____

9

Be the Coach!

 1 hour

Module 9 Objectives

In this module, you will have the opportunity to. . .

- **Get involved** by creating your own Coaching for Commitment Action Plan.
- **Discover** your new definition of coaching.
- **Commit** to making the shift, celebrating your successes, and staying on your coaching journey.

There's a fine line between who you are and who you want to be!

Commit to the Shift

How will I know I made the shift?

What **"trick"** will I commit to doing before each coaching conversation so that I know I made the shift to the coach role?

My trick. . .

_____

_____

_____

_____

_____

_____

What was my biggest ah-ha when playing the *coach role*?

_____

_____

_____

_____

_____

_____

What is my biggest challenge for implementing or using the *coach role*?

_____

_____

_____

_____

_____

_____

_____

"Successful coaching takes concentrated mental energy and effort that is draining yet revitalizing at the same time. Coaching is work!"

My Coaching for Commitment Action Plan

Name: Today's Date:
                                                             10 = Right on track 1 = Not on track

How would I rate myself on the following:

My use of the Coaching for Commitment   10 9 8 7 6 5 4 3 2 1
approach and skills

My ability to create a Coaching Culture   10 9 8 7 6 5 4 3 2 1

In terms of coaching, I would like to:
• **keep** doing:

• **stop** doing:

• **start** doing:

My current reality versus my ideal is:

How big is my gap?

What would I like to have happen in the next six months regarding my Coaching for Commitment approach and/or skills? In the next year?

I plan to accomplish this by (be specific):

My biggest challenges in implementing my plan will be:

I can overcome these obstacles by:

I will know I have achieved my goals when:

Coaching Rediscovered

My new definition of coaching:

Coaching is. . .

_____

_____

_____

_____

_____

_____

_____

_____

_____

_____

_____

_____

_____

_____

_____

_____

_____

_____

_____

_____

_____

_____

_____

_____

_____

_____

Go. . .

The biggest ah-ha moment I experienced as a result of attending this workshop was. . .

_____

_____

_____

_____

_____

_____

_____

One takeaway I will commit to using back at work is. . .

_____

_____

_____

_____

_____

_____

_____

My proudest accomplishment during this workshop was. . .

_____

_____

_____

_____

_____

_____

Resources

Thirty-Five Great Coaching Questions

Coach's Notes

Performance Coaching Worksheet

Coach Evaluation (Observer Form)

My Coaching for Commitment Action Plan

InDiCom Coaching Culture Guide

Quick Reference Guide

Thirty-Five Great Coaching Questions

1. How are things going?

2. How are you going to make that happen?

3. How can you be genuine/authentic in your response?

4. How can you influence this?

5. How do you feel about that?

6. How do you get the best out of people?

7. How do you let them know?

8. How has that gotten in your way?

9. How is that working for you?

10. How is this messing with your values? (Or rephrase the question and name the value.)

11. Tell me about your role model(s)? (Tie into changing behaviors.)

12. Tell me more.

13. What advice would you give someone in your shoes?

14. What are you afraid of?

15. What are you dependent on?

16. What assumptions are you making?

17. What does the ideal look like?

18. What is draining you/your team?

19. What is the best you can hope for?

20. What is the cost of that action/inaction/behavior?

21. What is the first thing you are going to do?

22. What is the worst question I could ask you right now?

23. What makes you say/think that?

24. What one word describes where you are at now? (Ask with Question 25.)

25. What one word describes your ideal?

26. What should you be modeling?

27. What should you be paying attention to?

28. What should your role be?

29. What three words do you want people to use when describing you? (Ask with Question 30.)

30. What do you need to do to live those three words?

31. What would you do if you did know? (Use when PBC responds with "I don't know.")

32. What would you do if there were no rules? (You can negotiate from here.)

33. What would you like to talk about?

34. What would your best friend/someone you admire tell you to do?

35. What is the underlying emotion you are feeling?

Coach's Notes

Use this as your guide for conducting your coaching conversations and capturing notes.

Name (PBC):   **Coach:**   **Date:**

	Shift to Coach Role!

InDiCom Coaching Model	**INVOLVE** Purpose and Expectations PBC accepted ownership Identified gap **DISCOVER** Root causes (core issues) PBC's ideas and solutions **COMMIT** PBC's plan of action Roadblocks/obstacles discussed PBC's recap Follow-up plans

	CHALLENGE	**LISTEN**	**ENCOURAGE**	**ASK**	**REFINE**
CLEAR	Request Reality Check	Story Telling Benefits of Silence	Validate Celebrate	Coaching Questions Powerful Statements	Two-Words Metaphors

Notes for Next Meeting	Remember to ask about during the next session: Key areas PBC is working on:

Performance Coaching Worksheet

PBC: **Coach:**   **Date:**

Use this form to prepare for your performance coaching conversations, when you bring the *why* ("*Why* are we having this conversation?") to the person being coached (PBC).

COACH'S OPENING. . .

Why is this conversation necessary? (Be specific.) How will I introduce it?

What does the PBC need to know about the situation and my expectations? (Most recent behavior versus expectations.)

What is the impact of the PBC's behavior on him or her, on me, the team, and/or the company?

How will I shift ownership so that the PBC owns the problem, gap, or issue? What question can I start with?

BEING FULLY PREPARED. . .

When and where will the coaching take place?

How will I eliminate distractions?

What will I say to establish and maintain trust?

How will I set the PBC at ease?

What is my ideal outcome? (If not ideal, what is the best I could hope for?)

How will I react if the PBC doesn't agree with my assessment?

If necessary, how will I depersonalize the situation?

What can I say to reduce resistance and/or remain focused on the future?

Are there things I need to own up to? (Was I unclear? Is there an unusually heavy workload?) How can I communicate those things?

What positive feedback or acknowledgements will I use?

What is my timeline for visible progress?

What are my follow-up needs/commitments from the PBC?

What documents or data must be gathered before the meeting?

Additional Comments:

Evaluating Your Coaching

If you would like to find out just how well you are doing at coaching, ask!

The following is a quick tool that can be used either for self-evaluation or it can be given to those you coach in order to help you assess your coaching progress. One reminder: the coach approach can be new and different for the PBC at first. It is recommended that you not use the following evaluation with the PBC until your PBC understands Coaching for Commitment. For more on introducing the topic of coaching, pick up a copy of the *Coaching for Commitment Discussion Guide* (sold separately).

If you are a coach using this tool as a self-evaluation, you will need to be extremely objective. Think of your coaching session as if you had been a third-party observer and rate yourself accordingly. If you are the observer, assess how the coach performed, not the specific content or outcome of the coaching conversation.

Rate the skills of the coach and the extent to which the coach demonstrated the behavior indicated. Be objective and capture examples where possible.

COACH EVALUATION

Observer: Rate the skills of the coach, not the topic of the coaching conversation. Using the scale below, rate the extent to which the coach demonstrated the behavior indicated. Be objective in your evaluation and capture examples where possible

5 = To a Great Extent	3 = Somewhat	1 = Not Really

InDiCom Coaching Model   Rating

	Rating
Coach was attentive to the needs of the PBC?	5 4 3 2 1
Coach focused on clarifying the purpose?	5 4 3 2 1
Coach kept the ownership of the situation on the PBC?	5 4 3 2 1
Coach identified the gap?	5 4 3 2 1
Coach allowed autonomy and innovation in generating solutions?	5 4 3 2 1
Coach resisted fixing the problem/situation for the PBC?	5 4 3 2 1
Coach facilitated the PBC's creation of an action plan?	5 4 3 2 1
Coach discussed barriers and obstacles?	5 4 3 2 1
Coach had the PBC provide the recap?	5 4 3 2 1
The conversation felt natural.	5 4 3 2 1

CLEAR Coaching Skills

Challenge: Coach used intuition to stay in tune with the PBC?	5 4 3 2 1

Bonus: Coach presented a *request* or *reality check?* Yes or No (circle one)

Listen: The coach heard and understood what was being said?	5 4 3 2 1
Encourage: Coach used validate and celebrate statements?	5 4 3 2 1
Ask: Coach asked coaching questions (not leading or rapid fired)?	5 4 3 2 1
Refine: Coach kept the conversation on track and focused on the PBC's accountabilities?	5 4 3 2 1

Bonus: Coach used *two-words* or metaphor? Yes or No (circle one)

Additional Comments:

Interpreting Your Scores

If you are planning to give this evaluation to more than one person, total the scores on each evaluation and then take the average so that you may easily refer to the following key:

A score of 66 to 75 indicates you are doing an excellent job Coaching for Commitment! Keep up the great work and come back to the book to brush up once in a while.

A score of 56 to 65 indicates that you are far above average in your coaching. You can still benefit from more practice. Keep this book close by as a reference guide.

A score of 46 to 55 indicates that you are doing an average job coaching. There is still work to be done! Lots of practice and refreshing yourself on Chapters 5, 6, and 7 will benefit you greatly. Find a coaching buddy—someone who will read this book, help you apply the model and skills, and practice with you. Redo your assessments every two or three months or until you see marked improvement in your scores.

A score of 36 to 45 indicates that, although you are likely trying your best, you are struggling with Coaching for Commitment. Don't give up! Start by re-reading Chapters 2, 5, 6, 7, and 8, as well as any others that reflect where you believe you are lacking in your skills or delivery. Also revisit Appendix D (Your Personal Coaching for Commitment Plan) and find yourself a coaching buddy—someone who will read this book, help you apply the model and skills, and practice with you. Search yourself to see whether this is a method you can truly embrace. If so, ask your team or peers to help you with the skills you are trying to master. Remember that being *egoless* is the key to great coaching! Redo these assessments every month until you see marked improvement in your scores. Move to every three months after that until your scores are consistently above 56.

A score of 35 or below indicates that you may need more than just practice and continued reading, although these are a great start. Ask yourself whether you are really ready to be a coach and are committed to being the best one you can be. If your answer is yes, then do everything you can to follow through with that commitment. Create an action plan that outlines how you can move forward to your goal of Coaching for Commitment. Within that plan, create specific and measurable goals and timeframes. Hold yourself to them and, if you are truly serious, enlist the ongoing help of another coaching professional (possibly an external executive coach) or your HR manager. Find a buddy—someone who will read the book *Coaching for Commitment* (3rd ed.), help you apply the model and skills, and practice with you.

Ask the person to evaluate you using this tool every time you practice coaching until you show marked improvement. Continue using the tools from Coaching for Commitment and push yourself by finding "What's in it for you."

It is rare, but some people are truly not cut out for coaching. Others just don't believe in it. Whether you decide to master the art of coaching or not is up to you. Whatever you decide to do, in whatever role you play, give it your best.

My Coaching for Commitment Action Plan

Name: Today's Date:

                                                   10 = Right on track   1 = Not on track

How would I rate myself on the following:

My use of the Coaching for Commitment   10 9 8 7 6 5 4 3 2 1
approach and skills

My ability to create a Coaching Culture   10 9 8 7 6 5 4 3 2 1

In terms of coaching, I would like to:
- **keep** doing:

- **stop** doing:

- **start** doing:

My current reality versus my ideal is:

How big is my gap?

What would I like to have happen in the next six months regarding my Coaching for Commitment approach and/or skills? In the next year?

I plan to accomplish this by (be specific):

My biggest challenges in implementing my plan will be:

I can overcome these obstacles by:

I will know I have achieved my goals when:

InDiCom Coaching Culture Guide

The stages and goals of the InDiCom coaching model (see below) provide a process for creating your Coaching for Commitment Culture action plan. The guide consists of stage-specific questions. Answer these questions from a perspective that makes them applicable to your world. Although you can complete this guide individually, for best results, complete it with your team and/or stakeholders. Stakeholders are defined as those who are investing in the initiative or anyone (including employees) who has something to gain from its success. Start by creating your value proposition for coaching.

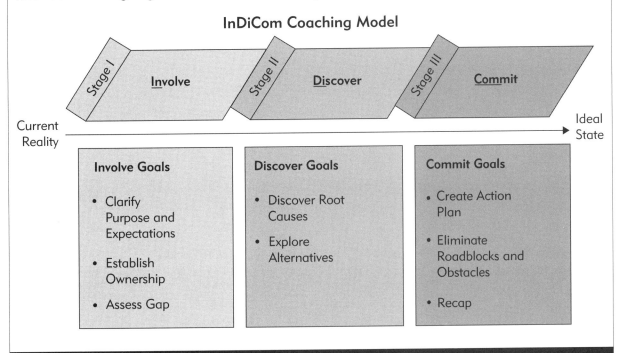

InDiCom Coaching Model

Stage I — Involve
Stage II — Discover
Stage III — Commit

Current Reality → Ideal State

Involve Goals

- Clarify Purpose and Expectations
- Establish Ownership
- Assess Gap

Discover Goals

- Discover Root Causes
- Explore Alternatives

Commit Goals

- Create Action Plan
- Eliminate Roadblocks and Obstacles
- Recap

Our Value Proposition for Coaching

What's in it for everyone involved?
What is our purpose in embracing coaching and creating a coaching culture?
What are we trying to achieve by creating a Coaching for Commitment Culture?
How will creating a Coaching for Commitment Culture change things?
What is the power of coaching?
What outcomes will be achieved by creating a Coaching for Commitment Culture?

(continued)

Stage I: Involve
Clarify Purpose & Expectations—Establish Ownership—Assess Gap

Project scope: Check the box that indicates the organizational level you are creating this plan for.

☐ Organization
☐ Region
☐ Division
☐ Department
☐ Team
☐ Other:

Who are the key stakeholders?

How is coaching currently used or portrayed?

What is the current perception of coaching (positive or negative)?

What is the ideal culture we are hoping to create (vision)?

What is the gap between current culture and ideal state?

What are our expectations?

Stage II: Discover
Discover Root Causes—Explore Alternatives

What has contributed to the current culture?

What does living the ideal culture look like?

What is our shared definition of coaching?

What perceptions (about coaching) need to be validated or dispelled?

What shifts need to occur in order to accommodate a new culture?

What needs to happen in order for us to support our value proposition?

What support do we need? From whom?

If needed, what is our redefined gap?

What research do we need to do?

What do the stakeholders need to know?

What do we need from our stakeholders?

Stage III: Commit
Create Action Plan—Eliminate Roadblocks & Obstacles—Recap

How will we get what we need from our stakeholders?

How do we move forward to reach our goals?

What steps should we include in our action plan (short term & long term)?

How will we begin to close our gap?

How will we create a common coaching language?

How will we dispel current perceptions (if applicable) so coaching is viewed with positive intention?

How will we teach the coaching concepts (model and skills) to others?*

Who will be responsible for what steps?

Who do we need to present our plan to for buy-in?

What challenges will we face (and from whom)?

How can we overcome these challenges?

How will we keep the Coaching for Commitment culture alive?

How will we measure our success (and how often)?

How will we know when we have reached our ideal?

*A *Coaching for Commitment Discussion Guide* is available through Pfeiffer.

Quick Reference Guide

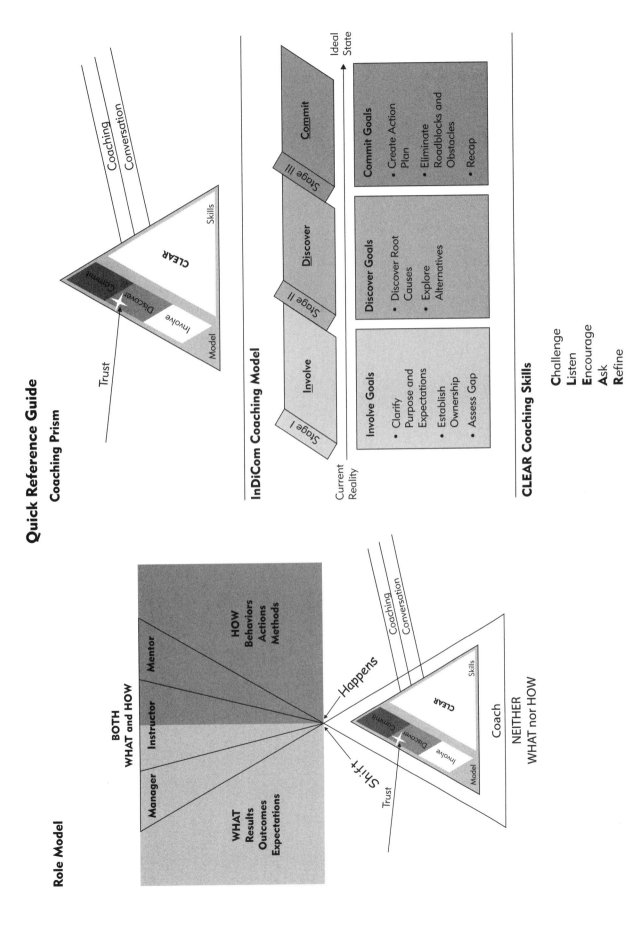

Coaching Prism

InDiCom Coaching Model

CLEAR Coaching Skills

Role Model

Carver, R.P., Johnson, R.L., & Friedman, H.L. (1970). *Factor analysis of the ability to comprehend time-compressed speech.* (Final report for the National Institute for Health). Washington, DC: American Institute for Research.

HighGain, Inc. (2000, June). Sssh! *Listen up! How to bring the critical skill of listening into your business.* Sebastopol, CA: Author.REFERENCES

Carver, R.P., Johnson, R.L., & Friedman, H.L. (1970). *Factor analysis of the ability to comprehend time-compressed speech.* (Final report for the National Institute for Health). Washington, DC: American Institute for Research.

HighGain, Inc. (2000, June). Sssh! *Listen up! How to bring the critical skill of listening into your business.* Sebastopol, CA: Author.

NOTES

NOTES

NOTES